Copyright © 2003 Carole Marsh

Permission is hereby granted to the individual purchaser or classroom teacher to reproduce materials in this book for non-commercial individual or classroom use only. Reproduction of these materials for an entire school or school system is strictly prohibited.

Published by
GALLOPADE INTERNATIONAL
800-536-2GET
www.gallopade.com

Gallopade is proud to be a member of these educational organizations and associations:

The National School Supply and Equipment Association
The National Council for the Social Studies
Association for Supervision and Curriculum Development
Museum Store Association
Association of Partners for Public Lands

BLACK JAZZ, PIZZAZZ, & RAZZMATAZZ BOOKS

Our Black Heritage Coloring Book

The Big Book of African American Activities

Black Heritage GameBook: Keep Score! Have Fun!
Find out how much you already know—and learn lots more!

Celebrating Black Heritage:
20 Days of Activities, Reading, Recipes, Parties, Plays, and More!

Mini Timeline of Awesome African American Achievements and Events

"Let's Quilt Our African American Heritage & Stuff It Topographically!"

The Best Book of Black Biographies

The Color Purple & All That Jazz!: African American Achievements in the Arts

"Out of the Mouths of Slaves": African American Oral History

The Kitchen House: How Yesterday's Black Women Created Today's
Most Popular & Famous American Foods!

Black Business: African American Entrepreneurs & Their Amazing Success!

OTHER CAROLE MARSH BOOKS

Meet Shirley Franklin: Mayor of Atlanta!

African American Readers—Many to choose from!

A WORD FROM THE AUTHOR

Trivia . . . but not trivial!

Dear Parent, Teacher, Librarian & other readers,

Perhaps this looks like an ordinary trivia book to you, but it isn't. "There are so many good, clever things in here — why don't you tell everyone!" one of my favorite booksellers (to schools) told me. So I am!

Please note the following goodies I've tried to sneak into this simple trivia book. (I think my bookseller friend thought they happened by magic, but I worked very hard to put them there!)

● The information is not just selected at random, but incorporates history, social studies, math, science, geography, language — and many other subjects children may be studying in school.

● The way the questions are worded is designed to get readers to stop and think — not just assume *this* is the question and so *this* is the answer. If they don't read clearly and follow directions, they may discover they have that backwards!

● The alternatives in the multiple choice answers are carefully selected to give the reader the opportunity to compare and contrast. You might be surprised to discover that your child does not know the difference between 1, .1 and .01. You'll learn a lot more from their answers than just if they know the answer!

● The silly answers, that leave little doubt as to the correct answer, are designed to give the reader confidence in answering questions. They need to learn to trust their own judgment and not read more, or less, into the questions than is there.

● I've intentionally chosen some questions that I think adults will miss! Why? Because it makes kids laugh + they see that there is always something new to learn, even after you're all grown up.

These are just a few of the ways I've tried to make "trivia" = fun + numerous educational experiences at the same time. I hope you think it "works" and will try some of my other not so trivial trivia books!

Carole Marsh

Hello boys and girls! My name is Ms. Smart. Let's get started!

1. Who was Mary McCleod Bethune?

    a) advisor to four presidents
    b) division administrator of National Youth Administration
    c) founder and president of Bethune-Cookman College in Daytona Beach, Florida
    d) all of these
    e) none of these

2. How long did America practice slavery?

    a) about 250 years
    b) about 25 years
    c) about 2500 years

3. Until recent years, who wrote most slave history books?

    a) black writers
    b) white writers
    c) there were no books

4. In what year were slaves set free by law?

    a) 1586
    b) 1865
    c) 1658

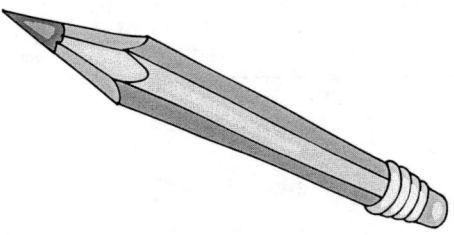

Answers: 1. d; 2. a; 3. b; 4. b

Hello boys and girls! My name is Mr. Wisdom. You're off to a great start!

5. Edward Bouchet was:

   a) an elected member of Phi Beta Kappa
   b) the recipient of a doctorate degree from Yale University
   c) a black man
   d) all of the above
   e) none of the above

6. Approximately how many blacks served in the Union Army during the Civil War?

   a) 8,000
   b) 18,000
   c) 180,000

7. Who was the first African American to win a Nobel Peace Prize?

   a) Dr. Martin Luther King, Jr.
   b) Dr. Ralph Bunche
   c) The Rev. Dr. Ralph David Abernathy

8. What do the initials N.A.A.C.P. stand for?

_____ _____ _____ _____

HOW ARE YOU DOING SO FAR? YOU CAN KEEP SCORE, YOU KNOW! ONE POINT FOR EACH RIGHT ANSWER.

Answers: 5. d; 6. c (37,000 lives were lost and 17 won the Congressional Medal of Honor.) 7. b; 8. National Association for the Advancement of Colored People

9. When Alex Haley wrote his bestselling book *Roots*, he was writing about:

a) a black family who raised most of their food in the garden
b) his family's roots back in Africa
c) troubles he had because of his love of money, the so-called "root of all evil"

10. Sisters Venus and Serena Williams are professional _____ stars!

a) basketball   c) soccer
b) tennis   d) volleyball

11. Malcolm X, who founded the Organization for Afro-American Unity in 1963, was a leading spokesman for:

a) black rights
b) black service
c) black pride

12. Which person is the bestselling American black novelist?

a) Paige Turns
b) Harriet Beecher Stowe
c) Frank Yerby

ASK THESE QUESTIONS AROUND THE KITCHEN TABLE AT DINNER. KEEP SCORE FOR EVERYONE. GIVE YOUR YOUNGER BROTHERS AND SISTERS A HINT!

Answers: 9. b; 10. b; 11. c; 12. c (What did he write?)

Can you feel your brain cells moving yet? Mine are going crazy already!

13. Bill Cosby, the father of one of America's favorite television families, was born in:

a) Chicago
b) Philadelphia
c) New York City

14. General Colin Powell became the first black to serve in what top U.S. government position.

a) Chairman of Joint Chiefs of Staff
b) U.S. President
c) Secretary of Defense

15. Actor and comedian John Sanford changed his professional name to:

a) Eddie Murphy
b) Bill Cosby
c) Redd Foxx

16. Who is the black main character in a play by William Shakespeare?

a) Romeo
b) Othello
c) Macbeth

Answers: 13. b; 14. a; 15. c; 16. b (What was the play titled?)

17. He was a legendary black man who was so strong that he could outwork a steam drill. He died with a hammer in his hand:

   a) John Henry
   b) Casey Jones
   c) Stevie Wonder

18. Joel Chandler Harris created this famous "Uncle," who spun tales about animals to entertain a white boy on a plantation:

   a) Uncle Tom
   b) Uncle Sam
   c) Uncle Remus

19. William Wells Brown, novelist and dramatist, was the first African American to:

   a) publish a novel
   b) write a screenplay
   c) work as a columnist

20. In 1963, Sidney Poitier became the first black person to win an Academy Award for Best Actor. Name the movie for which he received it:

   a) *Guess Who's Coming To Dinner?*
   b) *Lilies of the Field*
   c) *A Patch of Blue*

WHO IS YOUR FAVORITE AFRICAN AMERICAN WRITER?

Answers: 17. a; 18. c; 19. a; 20. b

Did you ever learn so much in *one* book? Good gracious!

21. In 1960, this NBA Rookie of the Year became the leading team scorer for that year and for the next six years:

a) Kareem Abdul-Jabbar
b) Oscar Robertson
c) Wilt Chamberlain

22. The Spingarn Medal is awarded annually by the N.A.A.C.P. to a black American for:

a) highest achievement
b) patriotism
c) political contribution

23. Benjamin Banneker was an inventor, astronomer, mathematician, and gazetteer. He served on the commission that laid out the plans for which U.S. city?

a) New York City
b) Washington, D.C.
c) Atlanta, Georgia

24. This western fur trader found a northern California mountain pass that was later named for him:

a) Isaiah Dorman (Dorman Pass)
b) Benjamin Hooks (Hooks Pass)
c) James P. Beckwourth (Beckwourth Pass)

Answers: 21. c (On which teams did he play?); 22. a; 23. b; 24. c

25. Shirley Chisolm was the first black woman elected to:

a) public office
b) the House of Representatives
c) the U.S. Senate

26. George Washington Carver was a botanist, chemurgist, inventor, and educator. He revolutionized the Southern economy with his extensive experiments in:

a) soil building and plant diseases
b) farm automation
c) crop rotation
d) both a and c

27. Major U.S. city of which Thomas Bradley became the elected mayor in 1973:

a) Atlanta   b) Los Angeles   c) Boston

28. Painter Aaron Douglas became known as:

a) The Black Artist
b) the father of black American art
c) neither

USE THESE QUESTIONS FOR A BLACK TRIVIA GAME IN YOUR CLASSROOM! YOU HAVE THE AUTHOR'S PERMISSION TO COPY THEM. THEN YOU COULD CUT THEM UP AND PUT THEM IN A HAT – DRAW A QUESTION OUT. KEEP SCORE!

Answers: 25. b; 26. d; 27. b; 28. b.

29. Noted poet and first African American to win a Pulitzer Prize:

   a) Langston Hughes
   b) Paul Laurence Dunbar
   c) Gwendolyn Brooks

30. This 19th century U.S. Army interpreter was killed with General Custer at the Battle of Little Big Horn:

   a) Andrew F. Brimmer
   b) Isaiah Dorman
   c) Crispus Attucks

31. Inventor Henry Blair obtained patents in the 1800s for:

   a) the corn planter   c) neither
   b) the cotton planter   d) both

32. The bestselling, award-winning book, *The Color Purple*, was also a hit movie starring Whoopi Goldberg. The author is:

   a) Alice Walker
   b) Stephen Spielberg
   c) Richard Wright

ARE YOU ANSWERING ALL THESE QUESTIONS CORRECTLY? IF NOT, LOOK THEM UP IN A BOOK! THEN KEEP GOING THROUGH THE BOOK UNTIL YOU "MAKE A HUNDRED"!

Answers: 29. c; 30. b; 31. d (What would you like to invent?); 32. a

Feeling smart yet? You should be!

33. This lady served as Underground Railroad conductor and spy for the Union Army in the Civil War:

a) Phyllis Wheatley
b) Shirley Chisholm
c) Harriet Tubman

34. Black entrepreneur who started his own cookie company:

a) Wally Amos
b) Amos Fortune
c) Cooky Crumbles

35. From 1973 through 1976, this internationally famous singer won 3 out of 4 of the Grammy Awards for Male Pop Vocalist:

a) Lionel Ritchie
b) Stevie Wonder
c) Michael Jackson

36. In 1775, at the Battle of Bunker Hill, British commander Major John Pitcairn was shot and killed by:

a) Nat Turner
b) Wilson C. Riles
c) Peter Salem

Answers: 33. c; 34. a (His company makes Famous Amos Chocolate Chip Cookies!); 35. b; 36. c (Have you read about this story yet?)

©CAROLE MARSH/BLACK TRIVIA: THE AFRICAN AMERICAN EXPERIENCE A-TO-Z!/PAGE 13

37. Dr. Daniel Hale Williams is credited with which of the following?

 a) performing the first open heart operation
 b) founding Provident, Chicago's first Negro hospital
 c) being elected a fellow of the American College of Surgeons
 d) all of these
 e) none of these

38. This early civil rights leader went on to become a congressman and chairman of the House Committee on Education and Labor:

 a) Benjamin Mays
 b) Adam Clayton Powell, Jr.
 c) Bayard Rustin

39. Booker T. Washington, author of *Up From Slavery*, made his largest contribution in the field of:

 a) education   b) politics   c) medicine

40. Sojourner Truth was active as:

 a) a preacher
 b) an abolitionist
 c) fund-raiser for the Union Army
 d) advocate for black education
 e) all of these
 f) none of these

Answers: 37. d; 38. b; 39. a (He also founded the Tuskegee Institute); 40. e (What is an abolitionist?)

41. Poet Phyllis Wheatley was:

a) the first black woman to have her works published
b) the second American woman to have her works published
c) a and b
e) neither a nor b

42. The Montgomery bus boycott, led by the Rev. Dr. Martin Luther King, Jr., brought about the Supreme Court decision that declared:

a) racial segregation of buses is unconstitutional
b) racial segregation of public schools is unconstitutional

43. She became the first African American to win an Olympic gold medal at the Winter Games (Salt Lake City, 2002):

a) Jill Bakken
b) Vonetta Flowers
c) Marion Jones

44. After leading the most significant slave revolt in U.S. history, Nat Turner was:

a) stoned   c) burned at the stake
b) hanged   d) set free

WHAT CAREER WOULD YOU LIKE TO HAVE WHEN YOU GROW UP? WHAT SPECIAL CONTRIBUTION WOULD YOU LIKE TO MAKE?

Answers: 41. c; 42. a; 43. b; 44. b

Your teacher is going to be proud of you! I know we are!

45. Paul Robeson was not only an actor and concert musician. He also:

a) graduated first in his class at Rutgers University
b) identified with the Russian people
c) graduated from Columbia University law school
d) all of these
e) none of these

46. Former nurse Ruth Carol Taylor became the first African American female:

a) zookeeper   b) flight attendant   c) biologist

47. The first African American female _____ was Dr. Mae Jemison.

a) explorer
b) doctor
c) astronaut

48. Jackie Robinson of the Brooklyn Dodgers was the first black major league baseball player.

True or false? _____

WHAT AFRICAN AMERICAN ANCESTOR DO YOU ADMIRE MOST? WHAT CONTEMPORARY BLACK PERSON DO YOU ADMIRE MOST?

Answers: 45. d; 46. b — upup and away!!; 47. c; 48. True

49. Vanessa Williams was the first black:

a) Miss America
b) Miss Universe
c) Miss New York

50. Who was the first black boxer to hold the heavyweight championship longer than a decade?

a) Jack Dempsey   b) Louie Armstrong   c) Joe Louis

51. Cuban blacks first performed the rumba as a rural dance to symbolize:

a) farm chores
b) sailing
c) flying

52. African sailor who helped Christopher Columbus navigate the *Niña* ship and was the first black to land in the New World:

a) Sir Walter Raleigh
b) Prince
c) Pedro Alonzo Niño

HOW LONG IS A CENTURY? WHAT DO YOU THINK LIFE WILL BE LIKE FOR AFRICAN AMERICANS BY THE YEAR 2100?

Answers: 49. a; 50. c; 51. a; 52. c

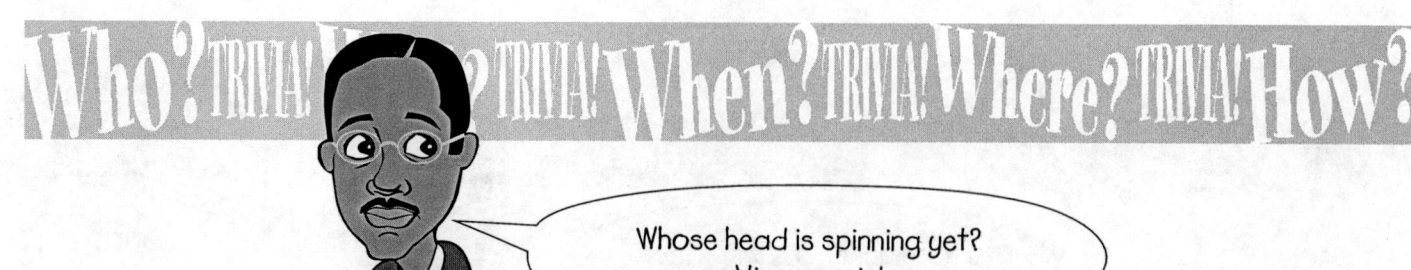

Whose head is spinning yet? Mine sure is!

53. The first black to be elected to the Hall of Fame for great Americans was:

a) Booker T. Washington
b) Harriet Tubman
c) George Washington Carver

54. Black explorer Matthew Henson discovered the:

a) Amazon rainforest
b) Dead Sea Scrolls
c) North Pole

55. Isabella Baumfree was the real name of:

a) Sojourner Truth
b) Harriet Tubman
c) Whitney Houston

56. Debi Thomas was:

a) an ice skater
b) a Miss America
c) the creator of Little Debi snack cakes

WHO WOULD YOU ELECT TO THE HALL OF FAME?

Answers: 53. a; 54. c; 55. a; 56. a

57. Gregory Hines is:

a) a basketball star
b) a dancer
c) a chef
d) a halfback

58. In 1883, a town was incorporated for blacks in:

a) Eatonville, Florida
b) St. Augustine, Florida
c) Miami, Florida

59. Althea Gibson was a famous black:

a) singer
b) tennis player
c) golfer
d) both b and c

60. Joseph Searles was the first black man to get a seat:

a) on a bus
b) at a lunch counter
c) on the New York Stock Exchange

WHAT DOES "INCORPORATED" MEAN?

WHAT DOES "LOVE" MEAN IN TENNIS?

Answers: 57. b; 58. a; 59. d; 60. c

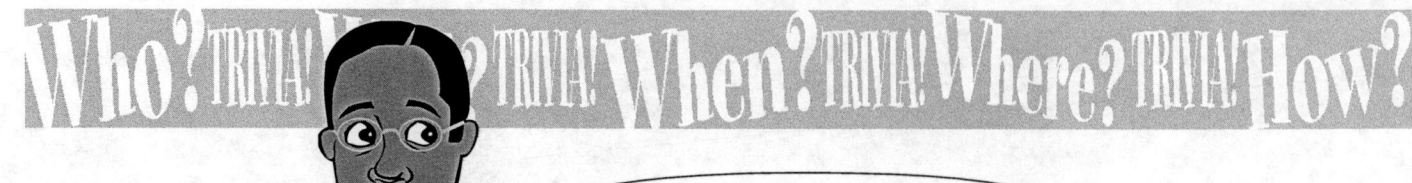

61. The first U.S. postage stamp to honor a black American was of:

a) Rosa Parks
b) Booker T. Washington
c) Dr. Martin Luther King, Jr.
d) George Washington Carver

62. The first organization to come out openly against slavery was:

a) the N.A.A.C.P
b) the Society of Friends
c) the Red Cross

63. In 1619, the first blacks in America arrived in:

a) North Carolina
b) Jamestown, Virginia
c) Boston Harbor
d) Charleston, South Carolina

64. Dr. Samuel Nabrit was the first black appointed to this U.S. commission:

a) Education
b) Defense
c) Atomic Energy
d) Housing and Urban Development

WHAT IS "BLACK HISTORY"? IS BLACK HISTORY REALLY "BLACK" HISTORY? WERE THE QUAKERS A BLACK GROUP? IF NOT, WHY DID THEY HELP THE SLAVES?

Answers: 61. b; 62. b – the Quakers!; 63. b – (as indentured servants); 64. c

You're doing so well! Did you study last night?

65. Dr. Percy Julian's extensive contributions were made in the area of:

a) peace
b) textiles
c) chemistry
d) economics
e) ecology
f) exobiology

66. In 1962, Martin de Porress was the first black from the Americas to be made:

a) a saint
b) a first baseman
c) free

67. Marcus Garvey advocated "back to _____":

a) Africa
b) basics
c) back

68. In 1968, Rev. Channing Phillips became the first black to ever be nominated for:

a) the U.S. Presidency
b) the Supreme Court
c) the Spingarn award

Answers: 65. c; 66. a; 67. a; 68. a – (by the Democratic Party)

Keep going you geniuses! I know you will finish on top!

69. Frederick Douglass was nominated as a presidential candidate in:

a) 1898   b) 1888   c) 1788

70. Black policeman William West once arrested:

a) Michael Jackson
b) President Ulysses S. Grant
c) Ku Klux Klan members

71. Thomy Lafon, born in poverty, became the first black philanthropist in America. A philanthropist:

a) pulls teeth
b) donates money to charities and others
c) instigates riots

72. The black music group Parliament played what type of music?

a) rap
b) classical
c) funk
d) reggae

START YOUR OWN COLLECTION OF BLACK TRIVIA. KEEP THE ITEMS IN ENVELOPES. MARK THEM ACCORDING TO CATEGORIES THAT INTEREST *YOU*... LIKE HISTORY, GEOGRAPHY, SPORTS, HUMOR, KIDS, FOOD, STARS, WOMEN... ANYTHING!

Answers: 69. b – (by the Republican Party); 70. b – What happened? Grant was arrested for driving his horse and buggy too fast. (Grant promoted the officer for doing his job so well); 71. b – He gave almost half a million dollars to blacks and whites; 72. c.

©CAROLE MARSH/BLACK TRIVIA: THE AFRICAN AMERICAN EXPERIENCE A-TO-Z!/PAGE 22

Wow! You students must have *some* teacher!

73. Jesse Owens won this many gold medals in the 1936 Olympics:

a) 2   b) 3   c) 4

74. In 1867, Howard University was founded in which major U.S. city?

a) Atlanta, Georgia
b) New York, New York
c) Washington, D.C.

75. Wilma Rudolph did not learn to walk until she was eight years old. At age 20, she was called:

a) a poster child
b) the world's fastest woman
b) a reindeer

76. Susie King Taylor, served with the First Regiment of the South Carolina Volunteers (the first black unit to fight in the Civil War) as a:

a) bugler
b) soldier
c) nurse

Answers: 73. c (In what events?); 74. c; 75. b – She won 3 gold medals in the 1960 Olympics!; 76. c – She was the first black army nurse in U.S. history.

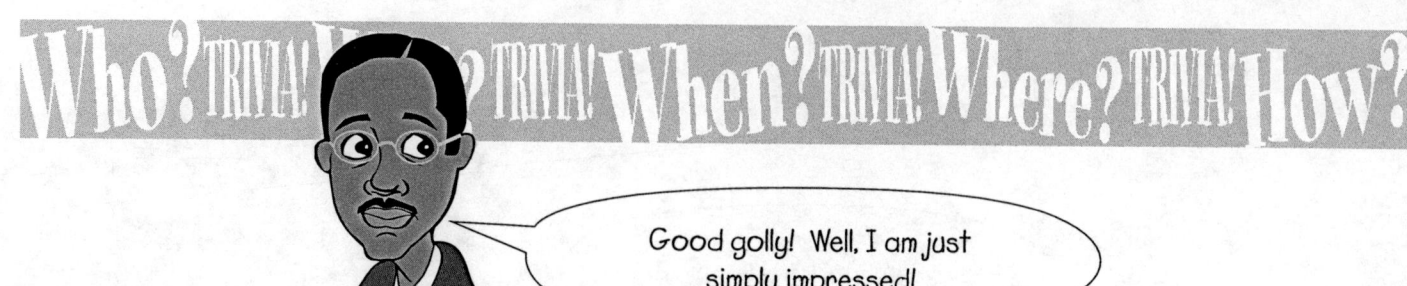

Good golly! Well, I am just simply impressed!

77. *La Tribune*, the first black *daily* newspaper in the U.S., was published in:

   a) Miami   c) Atlanta
   b) Chicago   d) New Orleans

78. "Lift every voice and sing" is the title and first line of:

   a) the Black National Anthem
   b) an old spiritual
   c) the Emancipation Proclamation

79. The word *Negro* comes from what language?

   a) African
   b) Spanish & Portuguese
   c) slang American

80. In 1848, William Alexander Leidesdorff became the first black American:

   a) airline pilot   b) cotton merchant   c) millionaire

WHERE CAN YOU FIND YOUR BLACK TRIVIA? THAT'S EASY! IT'S EVERYWHERE. ADD WHAT YOU LEARN IN SCHOOL EACH DAY. READ THE NEWSPAPER EACH NIGHT. LISTEN TO THE RADIO. ASK ADULTS. GO TO THE LIBRARY (YOUR LIBRARIAN WILL BE GLAD TO HELP YOU). FIRST YOU WILL HAVE TENS OF ITEMS, THEN HUNDREDS, THEN THOUSANDS! WOW!

Answers: 77. d – What was the name of the *first* black newspaper, published in 1827?; 78. a; 79. b Word origin dates back to a 15th century exploration of the African coast conducted by Portugal.; 80. c (Leidesdorff owned extensive lands, a hotel, and a steamboat. He was also the first black diplomat in the United States.)

81. Dr. Charles Hale established:

a) The First Black National Bank of New York
b) The American Red Cross Blood Bank
c) The African Food Bank

82. Amos Fortune founded:

a) a public library
b) a major corporation
c) a fortune

83. Which black female singer is known as the "Queen of Soul"?

a) Tina Turner
b) Diana Ross
c) Aretha Franklin

84. The first major public library to feature a collection of black studies, books, and materials was in:

a) New York City
b) Chicago
c) Atlanta

WHAT DID THE BLOOD BANK MEAN TO PEOPLE OF EVERY COLOR?

Answers: 81. b; 82. a (New Hampshire, 1795); 83. c; 84. a (the Harlem branch of the NYC Public Library).

85. The phrase *Jim Crow* refers to:

   a) an old minstrel character
   b) songs about birds
   c) set of segregationist laws
   d) both a and c

86. The term "the real McCoy" was originated by black businessman Elijah McCoy.

True or false? _____

87. Oliver Lewis was a black:

   a) entrepreneur
   b) politician
   c) fighter
   d) jockey

88. Once an illiterate slave, James W. C. Pennington wrote:

   a) a Biblical commentary
   b) a dictionary
   c) the first major history of the black people

Answers: 85. d; 86. True – (slogan coined by his company); 87. d – He rode the horse Aristides, who won the first Kentucky Derby!; 88. c (His book was titled *The Origin and History of the Colored People.*)

I'll bet you kids could write your own book about black history!

89. Walter Jackson was the first black to do this:

   a) become governor
   b) cross the Atlantic
   c) mine gold

90. The city that Jean Baptiste Point du Sable founded was:

   a) Chicago
   b) Harlem
   c) New Orleans

91. Dr. John Rock coined the term:

   a) *Black Power*
   b) *Black is Beautiful*
   c) *Back to Africa*

92. Slavery existed in Africa.

   True or false?

   _____

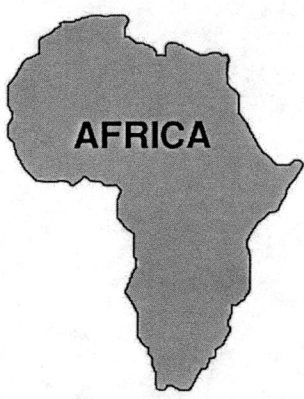

Answers: 89. c (California, 1849); 90. a; 91. b; 92. True – Both slaves and slave owners were black!

Hey! You with the pencil! You're almost there! Keep going strong!

93. Andrew Young was the first black U.S. ambassador to:

a) Africa
b) Canada
c) the United Nations

94. In 2002, this black athlete became the youngest golfer to win 8 PGA major titles:

a) Arnold Palmer
b) Jack Nicklaus
c) Tiger Woods
d) Ben Hogan

95. *Brown v. Board of Education*, which ended segregation in public schools, is associated with what Kansas town:

a) Tulsa
b) Topeka
c) Dallas
d) Albany

96. The year of the "March on Washington":

a) 1936
b) 1963
c) 1983

Answers: 93. c; 94. c; 95. b; 96. b

Look at all the smart kids in here!

97. Leader of a new goal to use the term "African Americans" instead of "blacks":

a) Malcombe Forbes
b) Al Sharpton
c) Jesse Jackson

98. Which state was the first to legally abolish slavery?

a) Vermont
b) Massachusetts
c) Virginia

99. Six year-old _____ became the first black child to desegregate a white school in America.

a) Ruby Bridges
b) Studee Harder
c) Maggie Lena Walker

100. Black History Month was created by black historian:

a) Carter G. Woodson
b) Booker T. Washington
c) Nat Turner

Answers: 97. c; 98. a; 99. a; 100. a (He first called the celebration Negro History Week)

©CAROLE MARSH/BLACK TRIVIA: THE AFRICAN AMERICAN EXPERIENCE A-TO-Z!/PAGE 29

Here's some BONUS questions for you!

 The Black Muslim religion was founded by:

a) Elijah Muhammad
b) Muhammad Ali
c) neither
d) they are the same person

 In 1983, Guion S. Bluford was the first black to represent America:

a) in World War I
b) in space
c) in the movies

 Jazz artist who received the Grammy Award for Female Vocalist in 1962:

a) Ella Fitzgerald
b) Lena Horne
c) Dionne Warwick

 In 2000, President George W. Bush appointed Condoleezza Rice to the post of:

a) Secretary of State
b) First Lady
c) National Security Advisor

Answers: B1. a; B2. b; B3. a; B4. c

©CAROLE MARSH/BLACK TRIVIA: THE AFRICAN AMERICAN EXPERIENCE A-TO-Z!/PAGE 30

Congratulations! You made it!

Bonus 5. A. Philip Randolph founded the:

a) Negro American Labor Council
b) Brotherhood of Sleeping Car Porters
c) both of these

Bonus 6. Actress and model Halle Berry became the first African American to win an Oscar for:

a) Best Actress
b) Best Supporting Actress
c) Prettiest Face

Bonus 7. This black military hero served America as a general in the Persian Gulf War:

a) Colin Powell
b) Norman Schwartzkopf
c) Benjamin O. Davis

Bonus 8. I know:

a) more about black trivia than I thought
b) less about black trivia than I thought

Answers: B5. c (How important were these organizations?); B6. a; B7. a; B8. ?!

Official
BLACK TRIVIA
Certificate

Presented to:

_____

This certificate verifies that the above named is officially an intellectual of The African American Experience!

Signature   Date

_____   _____